PORT SINGLE WINDOW SYSTEMS IN AFRICA

CRITICAL SUCCESS FACTORS AND LESSONS FROM THE PORT OF ABIDJAN

DR. DAGO ALAIN GOHOMENE

CONTENTS

ACRONYMS

1. **AACE** – African Association of Customs Experts
2. **ASEAN** – Association of Southeast Asian Nations
3. **ASYCUDA** – Automated System for Customs Data
4. **BOT** – Build-Operate-Transfer
5. **CSW** – Customs Single Window
6. **DGAMP** – Direction Générale des Affaires Maritimes et Portuaires
7. **EDAU** – Electronic Declaration of Advance Usage
8. **ETA** – Estimated Time of Arrival
9. **ETD** – Estimated Time of Departure
10. **GUCE** – Guichet Unique du Commerce Extérieur
11. **GUCE-CI** – Guichet Unique du Commerce Extérieur de Côte d'Ivoire
12. **ICT** – Information and Communication Technology
13. **IMO** – International Maritime Organization
14. **IPCOEA** – Improvement of Port Customs and Operations Efficiency in Africa
15. **MSW** – Maritime Single Window

16. **NSW** – National Single Window

17. **PAA** – Port Autonome d'Abidjan

18. **PCS** – Port Community System

19. **PPP** – Public-Private Partnership

20. **RFCV** – Request for Value Certificate

21. **SWS** – Single Window System

22. **UN/CEFACT** – United Nations Centre for Trade Facilitation and Electronic Business

23. **UNECE** – United Nations Economic Commission for Europe

24. **UNNExT** – United Nations Network of Experts for Paperless Trade and Transport in Asia and the Pacific

25. **WCO** – World Customs Organization

FOREWORD

The modern maritime industry is undergoing a profound transformation, driven by digitalization and the need for more efficient trade facilitation mechanisms. Among the most impactful innovations is the Single Window System (SWS), which streamlines port operations, enhances transparency, and reduces trade barriers. This book is a timely and significant contribution to the discourse on port digitalization, offering both theoretical insights and practical applications, with a particular focus on the Ivorian Port of Abidjan.

As ports worldwide strive to improve efficiency and comply with international trade regulations, the implementation of an effective Port Single Window is no longer optional — it is imperative. However, the journey toward a fully functional SWS is fraught with challenges, including governance issues, stakeholder alignment, and technological adaptation. By drawing from empirical research and real-world case studies, this book provides a comprehensive roadmap for policymakers, port authorities, and trade professionals navigating the complexities of SWS deployment.

The depth of analysis in this work highlights the critical factors that determine the success of a Single Window, such as political will, regulatory frameworks, and inter-agency collaboration. More importantly, it offers practical recommendations that can guide ports in developing countries as they pursue digital transformation in trade facilitation.

With its rigorous research and insightful perspectives, this book is an essential resource for scholars, industry practitioners, and decision-makers committed to shaping the future of maritime trade. I hope this work will inspire further innovation and strategic thinking in the field of port digitalization and trade facilitation.

Dr. Paul MANLAN
Consultant Trainer, Expert in
International Trade and Logistics

PREFACE

The global maritime and trade landscape is undergoing rapid transformation, driven by technological advancements and the need for greater efficiency in port and trade operations. Central to this transformation is the concept of the Single Window System (SWS), a pioneering solution that integrates multiple stakeholders to simplify and harmonize processes for international trade facilitation. This book delves into the critical elements of the SWS, exploring its theoretical underpinnings, implementation challenges, and practical applications with a focus on the Ivorian port of Abidjan.

The Port Single Window serves as a vital enabler for enhanced trade competitiveness, reducing costs, improving transparency, and fostering collaboration among stakeholders. Yet, as illustrated in this work, its implementation is not without hurdles, ranging from governance and infrastructure issues to stakeholder resistance and legal challenges. By documenting the experiences and lessons learned from the port of Abidjan, this book offers valuable insights for policymakers, practitioners, and researchers seeking to implement or improve SWS in similar contexts.

Through rigorous analysis and practical recommendations, this book contributes to the growing body of knowledge on trade facilitation in developing economies. It underscores the importance of government support, stakeholder engagement, and robust ICT infrastructure while addressing the nuances of local political, legal, and socio-economic conditions.

It is my hope that this book serves as both a reference and an inspiration for those working towards more efficient and sustainable trade practices, particularly in developing countries striving to integrate into the global trade system.

Ahou Florentine GUIHARD-KOIDIO
Expert in Port Information Systems

ACKNOWLEDGMENTS

First and foremost, I thank God for His grace, strength, and perseverance that sustained me throughout my PhD journey, from which this book is derived.

I express my sincere gratitude to my Director of Studies, Dr. Jana Ries, a technically adept and proficient researcher, and to my supervisor, Professor Mark Xu, a balanced academic and distinguished professional with deep expertise, particularly in e-government. Their constructive comments and insightful feedback have been invaluable throughout my research.

I am deeply grateful to the public and private stakeholders of the Ivorian Single Window System (SWS) at the Port of Abidjan, who participated in the interviews. Your contributions provided crucial primary and secondary data that significantly enriched this study.

A heartfelt thank you to my wife, Angela, whose unwavering moral support and care for our children allowed me the space and time needed to focus on my research. Your sacrifices and strength were instrumental in the completion of this journey.

To my parents, Mr. and Mrs. Rabe, I am truly thankful for your constant support and belief in me throughout this academic endeavor.

I extend special thanks to Colonel-Major Karim Coulibaly, Director of the Regional Maritime Academy of Abidjan (ARSTM), for facilitating access to the various stakeholders involved in my research.

I am also grateful to MFM Angré Region 3, Pastor Emmanuel Olukpero, and my fellow believers for their prayers, fellowship, and spiritual support. The church has been a wellspring of comfort and encouragement, and the peace of God has helped me overcome challenges I could not have faced alone.

Finally, I thank all my dear friends, brothers, and sisters who stood by me throughout this journey, especially during the challenging period of the COVID-19 pandemic. Your kindness and support made a profound difference.

INTRODUCTION

The Single Window System (SWS) was introduced by the United Nations Economic Commission for Europe in 2005 to streamline and facilitate international trade. In West Africa, many ports have adopted or are in the process of implementing SWS to enhance trade efficiency and position themselves as regional hubs. This initiative addresses longstanding challenges in customs and port operations, particularly the cumbersome administrative clearance procedures that have historically plagued the region.

Ports in West Africa have faced significant inefficiencies, especially in customs and administrative procedures. These inefficiencies often result in high operational costs, sometimes exceeding 70% of the cargo's value, as noted by Gikonyo et al. (2019). Such elevated costs deter shippers and impede regional economic growth. Congestion remains a pressing issue; for instance, in the Port of

Abidjan, vessels experience an average waiting time of 8.5 days; 3 days at anchor and 5.5 days at dock — highlighting the need for more efficient systems (PAA, 2020).

Implementing a fully paperless SWS can significantly reduce vessel waiting times by streamlining procedures for vessel reception and customs clearance, as suggested by Kabui et al. (2019). However, West African ports face challenges in achieving a fully paperless SWS due to issues related to ICT infrastructure and organizational hurdles, as reported by Dutta & Lanvin (2020). The involvement of multiple stakeholders with varying interests further complicates the implementation process (Jovic et al., 2021).

The Port of Abidjan has initiated steps toward establishing a maritime single window system. A needs assessment mission in Côte d'Ivoire laid the groundwork for this system, aiming to create a one-stop digital platform for information exchange among stakeholders involved in the arrival, stay, and departure of ships. Such a platform is expected to streamline procedures, saving both time and costs. Since January 1, 2024, it has been mandatory for all International Maritime Organization (IMO) member states to establish maritime single window systems in ports to enhance global shipping efficiency.

Despite these efforts, the implementation of SWS in West African ports remains complex and resource-intensive. It demands substantial investment, a shift in mindset, and strong political will (Keretho, 2013). The integration of ICT is crucial for automating processes and creating a paperless trading environment (WCO, 2015). Given the challenges, many governments opt for a phased approach, starting with limited implementations such as export declarations or specific areas like ports, before expanding the system's scope (WCO, 2015).

In Côte d'Ivoire, the ICT sector has seen improvements, but challenges persist. The country ranks 115th out of 134 economies in the Networked Readiness Index 2020, indicating a need for further development (Dutta & Lanvin, 2020). Issues such as low internet capacity and affordability hinder progress, with Côte d'Ivoire ranking 127th in terms of IT access affordability (Dutta & Lanvin, 2020). While mobile penetration is high, the adoption of ICT solutions like the SWS in the Port of Abidjan has been slower, partly due to a lack of determination among stakeholders for rapid implementation (PAA, 2020).

This book focuses on the implementation of SWS in developing countries, specifically in West Africa, using the Port of Abidjan as a case study. Unlike other maritime issues, the implementation of SWS in West African ports has not been extensively explored, particularly concerning the Port of Abidjan. Understanding the critical factors that negatively influence SWS implementation is essential. This knowledge will assist governments, the trade community, and stakeholders in adopting effective strategies for successful SWS implementation.

In summary, while the adoption of SWS in West African ports like Abidjan holds promise for enhancing trade efficiency, significant challenges remain. Addressing these issues requires a comprehensive understanding of the factors affecting implementation and a concerted effort from all stakeholders involved.

This book explores the Single Window System (SWS) and its role in trade facilitation, with a focus on the Ivorian experience. It begins with an overview of SWS and its benefits in streamlining trade, as well as a case study on the Port of Abidjan.

Chapter 1 defines key concepts, traces the evolution of SWS in international trade, and examines the role of technology, particularly in the Ivorian Port Single Window (PSW).

Chapter 2 highlights the benefits of SWS, including cost reduction, security, compliance, collaboration, and transparency.

Chapter 3 analyzes the Ivorian SWS Guichet Unique du Commerce Extérieur (GUCE) — its governance and comparison with the UN model.

Chapter 4 extends the analysis to West Africa, comparing SWS implementations, challenges, and best practices.

Chapter 5 draws lessons from the Ivorian case, offering strategic recommendations for developing countries. The conclusion synthesizes insights and future perspectives on trade digitalization.

Through case studies, comparative analyses, and practical recommendations, this book is a valuable resource for policymakers, port authorities, and trade professionals aiming to enhance trade efficiency through digital solutions.

METHODOLOGICAL APPROACH

The Single Window System (SWS) represents a relatively nascent innovation within West Africa, and more specifically in Côte d'Ivoire. This novelty has resulted in a notable scarcity of academic literature on the subject, creating a significant gap in knowledge that impacts both scholars and policymakers. Recognizing this void, the study adopted an interpretivist philosophical lens, which provided the foundational perspective for selecting an appropriate methodological framework. This interpretivist stance emphasizes the value of understanding complex phenomena through the subjective experiences of individuals directly involved, as well as through the contextual realities that shape these experiences (Kivunja & Kuyini, 2017).

Given the focus on exploring the intricate dynamics of SWS implementation at the Port of Abidjan, the study employed Stake's instrumental case study design (Stake, 2005; 2006). This methodological choice was pivotal in uncovering not only the "how" — the processes, practices, and strategies guiding SWS implementation — but also the "why" — the underlying factors contributing to delays in achieving a fully paperless system (Piekkari & Welch, 2018; Eriksson & Kovalainen, 2015; Gehman et al., 2018). By positioning the Port of Abidjan as the central case, the study sought to extract insights that could extend beyond the immediate context, offering lessons transferable to similar ports within the region.

A cornerstone of the methodology was the use of in-depth semi-structured interviews with fourteen key stakeholders (Appendix 1), all directly engaged with the SWS. This approach allowed for a nuanced exploration of their perspectives, shedding light on the multifaceted challenges and enablers of the system's implementation. The flexibility of the semi-structured format fostered rich, qualitative data, while still providing the consistency needed for cross-case analysis.

In addition to primary data collection, the study integrated third-party sources to strengthen the robustness of its findings through data triangulation (Stake, 2006; Boblin et al., 2013). This process ensured that the narratives drawn from stakeholder interviews were cross-verified with documentary evidence and other contextual data, thereby enhancing the credibility and depth of the analysis.

The decision to focus on qualitative inquiry was further reinforced by existing literature emphasizing the broader struggles faced by West African nations in transitioning to fully paperless SWS. Scholars such as Peterson (2017) and Kabui et al. (2019) highlight the persistent infrastructural, regulatory, and organizational hurdles that hinder these efforts. This study, therefore, positions itself within this critical discourse, aiming to deepen the understanding of how contextual factors shape the trajectory of SWS implementation.

Ultimately, the chosen methodological approach not only illuminated the complexities surrounding the Port of Abidjan's SWS but also offered a framework for examining similar initiatives across West Africa. By situating the research within an interpretivist paradigm and leveraging the depth of a case study design, this study contributes valuable insights to both academic scholarship and the practical considerations of port management and policy development.

CHAPTER 1:

DEFINITION OF KEY CONCEPT AND FEATURES OF SWS FOR PORTS

The Single Window System (SWS) has emerged as a transformative tool in modern trade facilitation, particularly within the maritime and port sectors. By streamlining administrative procedures and integrating digital technologies, SWS enhances efficiency, transparency, and compliance in global trade operations. This chapter explores the fundamental principles of SWS, its operational framework, and the key benefits it offers to stakeholders, including port authorities, shipping companies, and regulatory agencies. Through a detailed analysis, we will examine how SWS contributes to the simplification of procedures, reduction of delays, and overall improvement in port competitiveness.

1. Introduction to Single Window System

1.1. Definition and Evolution

The Single Window concept represents a groundbreaking governance model for international trade, transforming how regulatory processes are managed and delivered. According to the United Nations Economic Commission for Europe (UNECE), a Single Window, as outlined in UN/CEFACT Recommendation No. 33, is defined as:

"A facility that allows parties involved in trade to lodge standardized information and documents with a single-entry point to fulfill all import, export, and transit-related regulatory requirements."

This system is built on the principle of re-engineering traditional government structures to deliver seamless, efficient, and citizen-centric services. As Wang (2016) suggests, the Single Window philosophy allows governments to streamline service delivery by offering a unified interface for businesses and citizens. This approach reduces bureaucratic hurdles, enhances transparency, and fosters a more user-friendly experience.

The evolution of Single Window Systems reflects a significant shift in global trade practices, driven by technological advancements and changes in governance philosophy. Keretho (2013) emphasizes how innovations in Information Technology (IT) have unlocked new possibilities for improving regulatory frameworks, enabling greater efficiency and collaboration.

Beyond technology, the rise of Single Window Systems also signals a broader transition toward integrated governance models. These models are designed to make international trade more convenient, efficient, and aligned with the needs of modern economies. By combining cutting-edge technology with reimagined business architectures, Single Window Systems have emerged as indispensable tools for facilitating global commerce.

1.2. Importance of Single Window Systems in International Trade

Single Window Systems play a pivotal role in enhancing the efficiency of regulatory processes associated with international trade. By simplifying the complex, multi-agency organizational arrangements involved in service delivery, these systems promote transparency and streamline workflows for end users. As Joshi (2017) highlights, this efficiency leads to a significant reduction in transaction costs, benefiting businesses and fostering a more conducive trade environment.

The widespread recognition and adoption of Single Window Systems underscore their importance in trade facilitation. Key international organizations, including the United Nations Economic Commission for Europe (UNECE), UN/CEFACT, the World Customs Organization (WCO), the United Nations Network of Experts for Paperless Trade and Transport in Asia and the Pacific (UNNExT), and the Association of Southeast Asian Nations (ASEAN), have actively championed the implementation of these systems (Bajt & Duval, 2020).

Beyond their impact on trade, the principles underlying Single Window Systems have been applied in other areas of governance. For instance, local governments across the globe have introduced centralized platforms, such as web portals and kiosks, to streamline access to services like driver's licenses, parking permits, and benefits administration (Tessmann and Elbert, 2022). By consolidating these services into a single interface, governments minimize inconvenience for citizens, providing a one-stop solution that meets diverse needs efficiently and effectively.

In essence, Single Window Systems are not only transformative tools for international trade but also represent a broader movement toward integrated, citizen-centered governance. Their adoption simplifies regulatory processes, reduces costs, and promotes seamless interactions between stakeholders, making them indispensable in today's globalized economy.

1.3. The Role of Information Technology

The development and success of Single Window Systems are intrinsically linked to advancements in Information Technology (IT). IT serves as the backbone of these systems, enabling the creation of electronic interfaces that connect governments, businesses, and other stakeholders. These interfaces facilitate real-time data exchange and seamless integration across platforms, ensuring efficient and effective communication (Gikonyo et al., 2019).

In the realm of international trade, Single Window Systems operate as powerful trade facilitation tools. Their primary objective is to simplify and harmonize the processes involved in clearing goods across borders. By consolidating the services provided by multiple regulatory agencies, Single Window Systems manage value streams through advanced technology and organizational resources (MorosDaza et al., 2021).

A Single Window environment integrates IT systems from diverse sectors, including Customs, Port Authorities, Agriculture, Quarantine Services, and Food Safety. This comprehensive integration promotes efficiency, transparency, and coordination. The World Customs Organization (WCO, 2015) highlights four key themes that underpin the role of IT in Single Window Systems:

1. **Driving business simplification** – Streamlining processes to reduce complexity and eliminate redundancies.
2. **Coordinating regulatory controls** – Ensuring that various government agencies work in unison to enhance oversight.

3. **Facilitating trade through ICT** – Leveraging digital tools to enable faster, more secure trade processes.

4. **Enabling collaboration between Customs and other government agencies** – Enhancing partnerships and data sharing to ensure smooth operations.

Standardized communication interfaces are central to the effectiveness of Single Window Systems. These interfaces support the seamless electronic exchange of documents and data among traders, government agencies, and private stakeholders. Kabui et al. (2019) describe Single Window Systems as IT-driven business services, organized into non-overlapping categories and hierarchical structures.

In essence, IT transforms Single Window Systems into dynamic platforms that not only simplify regulatory processes but also enhance collaboration and transparency across the trade ecosystem. By harnessing the power of IT, these systems create a more connected, efficient, and responsive global trade environment.

1.4. Focus of This Book: The Ivorian Port Single Window System (SWS)

This book is the first of its kind to comprehensively address the challenges faced by developing countries in implementing Single Window Systems (SWS), with a particular focus on West Africa. By examining the case of the Ivorian Port Single Window, also known as the Guichet Unique Portuaire, at the Port of Abidjan, it sheds light on the complexities and opportunities inherent in applying SWS in a developing country context.

The Port of Abidjan serves as an ideal case study due to its significance as one of West Africa's busiest ports and its role as a gateway for trade across the region. Through a detailed exploration of the functionalities, implementation challenges, and operational features of the Ivorian Single Window System, this book offers valuable insights into the practical application of SWS in port environments.

In addition to its regional focus, this book provides a broader perspective that will be beneficial to researchers worldwide. It offers a unique resource for academics studying trade facilitation, digital transformation, and port operations, as well as practitioners involved in the design, implementation, and management of Single Window Systems.

The subsequent sections delve into the various types of Single Window Systems used in port environments, highlighting their key features and the critical factors that influence their success. By addressing the gaps in current literature and practice, this book aims to contribute to the global understanding of SWS and support efforts to enhance trade facilitation in developing regions.

2. Key Concepts and Features of SWS for Ports

According to Caldeirinha et al. (2022), Port single windows can be defined as a service that facilitates the exchange of standardized information and documents for the completion of all formalities related to the arrival, stay, and departure of vessels and the handling of goods from the arrival in port until their departure. The Ports Single Window Systems focus their objectives on information relating to ship calls in a country's ports, carriers, and/or shipping agencies, ports, and in general to all the stakeholders involved in processing the merchandise in ports (Moros-Daza et al. 2021).

The key stakeholders are not only the maritime and port authorities, shipping agencies, and carriers, but also customs, which is a critical stakeholder in the process of removing goods (Tijan et al., 2019). The main objective for all these stakeholders is to improve their process while encouraging the exchange of data and documents in an accelerated manner in addition to securing their revenues (Torlak et al., 2020). Depending on the scope of operations as defined by decision-makers, there are several types of Single Window Systems applicable to the maritime and port sector, as can be seen in **Table 1** below:

Table 1- Types and features of SWS applicable in port.

	Name of SWS	Mixed-Use (Functionalities)	Main Purpose / Use	Owner (Developm ent & Operation)	Stakehol ders
1	National Single Window System (NSW)	Yes, in some countries (e.g., CSW, MSW, PCS)	Managing and reporting national statistics to international institutions	National Governmen t	Only national, regional, or local authoritie s

2	Customs Single Window System (CSW)	Only national & local customs (including external on declarations & releases)	Customs clearance and collection of duties on imports, exports, or transit goods	National customs authority (developed and managed)	Local customs offices, carriers, shipping agencies, port authorities
3	Maritime Single Window System (MSW)	Yes, for customs, ports, health, & info used by carriers, ports & shipping agencies	Data on ships' calls in ports (ETA, releases, ETD) submitted by carriers, shipping agencies, or ports	National Port Authority; sometimes private sector involvement	Ports, carriers, shipping agencies
4	Port Community System (PCS)	No (some PCS go beyond traditional port use; may involve limited port terminals & shipping agencies)	Collects ship ETA, calls, handling & ETD information within the port area (e.g., port terminals, waiting berths), releases, and port dues	National and/or local Port Authorities (co-developed or operated by private contractors; owned/managed by local port authority)	Ports, port services, terminals, shipping agencies, and local customs with access to ship calls and ETA

Source: IPCOEA (2021)

The Customs Single Window system, the Maritime Single Window system (MSW), and the Port Community System (PCS) can be integrated into a national single window system. In other words, depending on the objectives and the financial capacities of the decision-makers, the

Customs Single Window system, the Port Community System (PCS), and the Maritime Single Window system can be implemented under a national single window system, also called Single Window System for foreign trade, which is the case with Cote D'Ivoire (CI).

On the other hand, in Europe, the emphasis is on the Maritime Single Window system (MSW).

Thus, the European Parliament and the European Council adopted Directive 2010/65/EU on 20 October 2010 regarding reporting requirements for ships arriving and departing from ports in the European Union (IPCSA, 2022). This legislation is more commonly known as the Reporting Formalities Directive (RFD). The RFD aims to simplify and harmonize administrative procedures related to maritime transport. The RFD required that Member States establish National Single Windows (NSWs) for the 14 reporting formalities outlined in its Annex, as of 1 June 2015, for ships arriving and departing from ports.

Since June 2015, ship arrivals at all German seaports have to be reported through the National Single Window, and parts of this information can be accessed by other EU Members on request via SafeSeaNet (a European-wide data exchange system designed to prevent accidents and pollution at sea and to reduce their consequences) (Tijan et al., 2019). A sustainable seaport business requires the involvement of stakeholders via MNSW, which the European Union is prioritizing. The reason for this is that the MNSW would provide a basis for sustainable maritime transport and business by harmonizing seaport business processes. Further, it could reduce administrative burden by harmonizing and reusing information.

According to Tijan et al. (2019), the interest that the European Union has in the MNSWs is linked to the fact that in an environment where there are many different information systems, information exchange among seaport stakeholders can be a bottleneck to achieving sustainable goals. It is unfortunate that, contrary to the European Union's wishes, all member states do not yet have access to SafeSeaNet. This was confirmed by a refit evaluation of the RFD initiated by the European Commission. According to the support study, the RFD's objectives were not met (or were partially met) (IPCSA, 2022).

The above illustrates the complexities surrounding the implementation of single window systems in ports. It is therefore pertinent to examine the factors influencing SWS implementation in developing countries' context using the port of Abidjan as a case study, which is the third largest port on the West African coast, behind Dakar and Lagos (PAA, 2021).

The different single window systems in Table 1 represent critical stages in implementing a national single window system in accordance with the single window road map developed by UNECE (2013). As part of the study, the single window road map will serve as a guide given that the Ivorian government uses it to implement its national single window, which includes the functionalities of a PCS, a customs single window system, and a maritime single window system. The following section provides an overview of the various single windows business models.

3. Three Single Windows Business Models

The success of Single Windows business models are highly dependent on the initial conditions of the environment (political, economic, social, technological), as well as a good identification and management of preconditions prior to the start of the project (Jovic et al., 2021). As a result, it remains imperative that a detailed estimate of the costs of implementing Single Window be provided. To achieve this, Tijan et al. (2019) suggested that the Single Window business model should include all stakeholders to effectively identify all needs (infrastructure, equipment, human resources, training, communication, etc.). Furthermore, the Single Window model must guarantee the balance between the three levels of funding: setting up, operating, and future sustainability (Aryee & Hansen, 2022). The three existing business models for SWS implementation are: the public financing model, the Public Private Partnership (PPP) model, and the concession model (AACE, 2017).

3.1. The Public Financing Model

Generally, this model is used when the funding for setting up, operating, and evolving the Single Window is provided by the government or a donor (Jovic et al., 2021). One of the reasons governments finance the various stages of a Single Window is to improve the foreign trade environment, especially through the facilitation of trade formalities and the good management of the Single Window (for instance, Kenya, Finland, South Korea, Sweden, the USA, Azerbaijan, Philippines, Tunisia) (AACE, 2017). In developing countries and least developed countries (LDCs), the absence of resources is one of the biggest risks associated with strong government involvement in the Single Window life cycle, as suggested by Peterson (2017). In such a situation, the Single Window could perform badly, and, where appropriate, private sector and donor involvement may be considered.

3.2. The PPP Model

In this model, Single Windows are set up as part of a public-private partnership (Jovic et al., 2021). The PPP is limited to the governance and management of the project. This mutually beneficial partnership aims to improve the competitive environment of foreign trade in countries such as Ghana, Hong Kong, Japan, Malaysia, Mauritius, Senegal, Singapore, Cameroon, Morocco, Congo, etc. (AACE, 2017). It is generally the case that Single Window services are cost-based under PPPs. However, these are often negotiated or approved rates aimed at balancing the operation. As a complement to other types of funding available, PPP offers the flexibility of calling on the Government as a stakeholder, or on donors based on the opportunity (IPCOEA, 2021). There are many PPP models espoused by the World Bank. However, for the purposes of the book, we focus on two sub-models, namely the concessionary model and the BOT model. The rationale for focusing on these two models is because they were used in the port of Abidjan for various projects, SWS inclusive (Delmon, 2015).

3.3. The Concession Model

The concession model is a sub-model of the PPP model (Delmon 2010). After a public service concession is awarded, the private sector may finance the Single Window's setup, maintenance, and operation (e.g., Germany, Dakosy) (Jovic et al., 2021). It is crucial that the operation is profitable in this process. As a result, the facility provides paid services. Generally, concessionaires are paid directly by users based on provisions in their contracts with concessioning authorities. In reality, administrations may have limited control over this type of contract. It is then possible for concessionaires to extend the concession period as well as the schedule of charges (IPCOEA, 2021). As a result, the Single Window concessionaire may charge high prices for services provided. For this reason, the government should strive to ensure that the Single Window is cost-effective by providing subsidies, if necessary, and mobilizing donors to provide financing.

3.4. Build Operate Transfer model

Xenidis and Angelides (2005) argue that the build-operate-transfer (BOT) is an approach for developing infrastructure projects. BOT is a project delivery technique that enables the fast realization of public works in case of a shortage of public funds. The process is inherent with risks, due mainly to the complexity and the number of stakeholders involved. However, Xenidis and Angelides (2005) assert that the identification, classification, and presentation of a comprehensive list of risks will provide BOT project practitioners with a useful tool in the effort to successfully set up a BOT concession agreement. Delmon (2015) also asserts that the BOT approach to describing Private Public Partnerships (PPP) for new project assets captures legal ownership and control of the project assets. Under a BOT project, the private company owns the project assets until they are transferred at the end of the contract to the government or public agency. The extant literature asserts that such BOT projects are financed by forming a Special Purpose Vehicle (SPV), which is independent of project developers or promoters. However, there are two major concerns derived from BOT project financing, namely:

1. The return on investment for developers is measured through equity returns instead of the value of the firm or of the project since they fund the project by holding a significant portion of the shares of the BOT firm.

2. The BOT firm is subject to bankruptcy before the completion of the project. However, In instances where the equity of the BOT firm is publicly placed, the project development failures are likely to cause political costs (Ho & Liu, 2002). Thus, in the instance of the SWS, the failures inherent in implementing the SWS have an impact on the political equity of the government.

3.5. Synthesis of business models

The various Single Window business models may be summarized as seen in Table 2:

Table 2 Summary of the various Single Window business models

	Business Models Financing	Set up	Operation Financing	Evolution Financing
1	Public financed model	Donors/Go vernment	Government	Donors/ Government
2	Concession model	Concessiona ire	Concessionai re	Concessiona ire
3	PPP model	Donor/Gov	Ad hoc entity	Ad hoc entity

Source: AAEC (2017)

4. Business Process Re-engineering for SWS Implementation

A Single Window aims to transform manual procedures into a more seamless and secure information channel without compromising the prerogatives of institutional stakeholders (Caldeirinha et al., 2022). Dematerializing procedures requires a business process analysis, which forms the basis for IT system performance and operation (Kapkaeva, 2021). Without analyzing and re-engineering existing processes, the benefits of a Single Window System will be minimal, and its flaws will persist (Moros-Daza et al., 2021).

Process analysis involves understanding the features of business processes and their interconnections, as well as clearly identifying the roles of each stakeholder (IP-COEA, 2021). In modeling processes, each element of a business process is illustrated with graphic notations, which depict the following points:

Activities that occur in a specific order, including decision points; stakeholders responsible for carrying out those activities; inputs and outputs defined for each activity, along with related criteria and rules; interconnections among stakeholders; and the flow of information throughout the company.

Quantitative indicators such as the number of stages, as well as the time and cost required to complete a specific business process, are crucial. The results of business process analysis can serve as a starting point for implementing trade facilitation measures such as the simplification of procedures, streamlining of document requirements, and alignment with international standards, automation of international trade transactions, and the creation of electronic documents for the Single Window. By implementing these trade facilitation measures, a fully functional Single Window System (SWS) can be established, highlighting the critical role of business process re-engineering in its implementation (Caldeirinha et al., 2022).

CHAPTER 2:

BENEFITS OF THE SWS

The implementation of the Single Window System (SWS) has revolutionized trade facilitation by enhancing efficiency, reducing costs, and improving transparency in global supply chains. This chapter explores the key benefits of SWS, focusing on its role in streamlining administrative processes, increasing compliance, and fostering better collaboration among stakeholders. Through real-world insights and case studies, we will examine how SWS has contributed to cost reductions, improved connectivity, and enhanced security, ultimately transforming the way businesses and regulatory agencies interact in international trade.

2.1. Cost Reduction

The findings from the interviews conducted for this book

paint a compelling picture of the transformative impact of the Single Window System (SWS). Traders, once burdened by cumbersome bureaucratic hurdles and costly delays, now navigate a streamlined, digitized landscape that significantly reduces compliance costs. The shift from manual to automated processes has not only expedited transactions but has also enhanced convenience, allowing businesses to operate with greater efficiency. The result is a tangible reduction in financial strain, a boost in productivity, and a trading environment that is more agile, transparent, and cost-effective.

"Our compliance costs associated with transportation/travel, time, administration (e.g., document preparation, photocopying), and telecommunication have been reduced or eliminated."

The interview with the stakeholders revealed that the compliance processes became more predictable and transparent.

"For instance, the number of physical movements between agencies by traders was eliminated, and those between banks have reduced a lot."

"Most traders and clearing agents have reported a reduction of over 50% in the cost to import."

There has also been a remarkable reduction or elimination of administrative costs related to the storage and retrieval of physical documents with the PAA.

It's also stated in the same interview that cost reduction was effective:

"We are very happy about the implementation of the single window system because it came to reduce the cost of doing business."

Based on the interviews, cost reduction has been the greatest satisfaction of the stakeholders, particularly traders (Importer/exporter).

2.2. Improved Connectivity and Security

The integration of diverse public and private stakeholders into the Single Window System (SWS) marks a significant milestone in modern trade facilitation. Key institutions, including the Ministry of Commerce, the Ministry of Agriculture, and insurance companies, now operate within a unified digital framework, transforming the once-fragmented permit issuance process into a seamless, interconnected system.

The implementation of the SWS was accompanied by a comprehensive business process review, which led to the simplification, streamlining, and harmonization of procedures. Documents were standardized and aligned, reducing redundancy and ensuring a more fluid exchange of information. Beyond mere efficiency, the system offers enhanced security and data integrity, allowing traders to submit documents electronically in a single, centralized platform.

A recent study by Mattei (2020) underscores the growing importance of digitalization in ports, highlighting that the push for technological advancement is not only fueled by the pursuit of efficiency but also by pressing concerns over safety and security. In this new era of trade, the SWS stands as a testament to how innovation can drive both operational excellence and resilience in global commerce.

"For example, a sea manifest submitted through the SWS is simultaneously and automatically made available to all stakeholders, including the Customs, for approval. The Ivorian SWS is more secure than the manual process because only authorized staff can access it."

An e-forex module has digitalized Exchange Authorization. This module allows the lifting of Exchange Authorizations or Exchange Commitments authorizing the payment of import invoices or the domiciliation of export invoices. It has a sub-module to monitor the repatriation of currencies obtained from operators' export sales through commercial banks.

2.3. Improved Compliance and Revenue Collection

As stated by Aryee et al. (2021), SWS in ports can improve customs clearance efficiency, increase government revenue, and reduce corruption associated with ports.

According to participants:

"Traders can no longer work outside of the system or find ways around the established payment procedures; the system enables easy detection of non-compliance and makes it easy to cross-reference from the system for the level of compliance of traders."

In the past, compliance among stakeholders was approached in a fragmented, ad hoc manner, lacking the cohesion necessary for seamless trade facilitation. The introduction of the Single Window System (SWS) has fundamentally transformed this landscape, establishing a structured and systematic framework that empowers stakeholders to effectively fulfill their regulatory mandates.

With the implementation of the SWS, adherence to statutory requirements has seen remarkable improvement. Revenue collection, once susceptible to loopholes and inefficiencies, is now more precise and enforceable, ensuring that traders meet their fiscal obligations without evasion. The system not only strengthens regulatory oversight but also fosters a more transparent and accountable trading environment.

Delving deeper into this transformation, stakeholders unanimously acknowledged the impact of the SWS. Their insights painted a compelling picture of a system that is not merely a tool for compliance but a catalyst for efficiency, fairness, and economic integrity.

"The SWS has reduced revenue leakage through minimal/elimination of cash transactions at the government agencies."

Generally speaking, the responses show that SWS is providing improved compliance and revenue collection.

2.4. Improved Collaboration Between Stakeholders

Beyond simply enhancing awareness of the roles and responsibilities of various public and private entities, the Single Window System (SWS) has served as a powerful catalyst for deeper collaboration and streamlined coordination. This is particularly evident among stakeholders whose functions are interdependent in the issuance of critical trade documents—a transformation well-documented by Putzger (2020).

Interviews with key players across the trade ecosystem underscore this progress. While challenges in stakeholder collaboration persist, there is unanimous agreement that the level of coordination has vastly improved compared to the pre-SWS era. In essence, SWS has not only facilitated compliance but has also forged stronger synergies between institutions, bridging gaps that once hindered seamless trade facilitation.

According to the participants, the collaboration has helped promote knowledge sharing among all the stakeholders. This improved collaboration between stakeholders is crucial for improving international trade.

2.5. Electronic Storage of Extensive Data

As highlighted by Kapkaeva et al. (2021), the Single Window System (SWS) serves as a pivotal mechanism for the seamless collection, processing, and storage of vast amounts of data generated by various stakeholders. This digital transformation has not only streamlined data management but has also reinforced the integrity and accessibility of crucial trade information.

Insights gathered from stakeholder interviews further underscore the profound impact of the SWS on data storage. Where once inefficiencies and fragmentation plagued information management, the system has introduced a structured, secure, and highly efficient framework. The consensus is clear: the implementation of the SWS has ushered in a new era of data reliability, ensuring that essential trade records are not only well-organized but also readily available to those who need them.

According to participants:

"In the past, the storage of data (physical files/records) was difficult for government agencies."

"Previously, it was difficult for government agencies to retrieve data efficiently, analyze and report it."

The SWS has offered secure, accurate, and efficient data repository and reporting capabilities, leading to real-time data updates among the public and private stakeholders. The SWS has allowed the stakeholders to generate reports with ease for prompt decision-making.

In this respect, a participant highlighted that:

"The SWS has enabled the country to have, on a real-time basis, a single source of data and trade facilitation statistics."

2.6. Enhanced Efficiency and Consistency

The Single Window System (SWS) stands as a dynamic and multifaceted information platform, designed to enhance real-time efficiency across every phase of the cargo handling process. From the intricate procedures of unloading and loading to the meticulous tasks of customs clearance and the seamless coordination of deliveries both within and beyond terminal confines, the SWS proves indispensable. As highlighted by Caldeirinha et al. (2020), traders and their facilitation agents have reported notable improvements in operational efficiency. Consequently, the time and expenses associated with securing permits, approvals, and essential documentation have been significantly reduced.

"The management team at the bank readily adhered to the SWS project and facilitated its adoption within it. The SWS brought celerity and efficiency to our work."

"Also, the fact that the majority of the stakeholders are integrated into the system facilitates the obtention of the information in a timely manner, which allows operational efficiency."

For public stakeholders like customs, this efficiency results in less fraud:

It has now become possible for us to view permits approved by the other Government Agencies online through the system. It is really good for us because it eliminates or reduces document falsification.

Interviews with stakeholders have revealed that the permits are available in real-time as soon as they are approved. The SWS has improved communication and sharing of documents between public and private stakeholders and government agencies. For instance, the freight forwarder is able to access all the permits and licenses issued by the Ministry of Commerce to their clients (Importers/exporters) on the SWS platform.

"This has entirely removed the need for the traders (Importers/Exporters) going from office to office, a requirement that existed before the advent of the SWS."

In addition,

"Most of the movement between public stakeholders for physical transfer of documents was eliminated through automation and business process re-engineering."

Through the interviews, it was also confirmed that the SWS helps improve risk management by the customs. According to participants:

"It became easy for the Customs to target and release cargo using the Risk Management Module in the SWS."

The Single Window System (SWS) empowers Customs authorities to meticulously profile cargo by evaluating various criteria, including the place of origin, the nature of the goods, and the historical records of importers and exporters. This targeted approach enables the identification of specific individuals or consignments, thereby minimizing disruptions to other stakeholders.

In Côte d'Ivoire, the implementation of the SWS has facilitated a significant reorganization among public and private stakeholders. By automating repetitive tasks that previously demanded substantial human intervention, the system has liberated the workforce to concentrate on more value-added activities, thereby enhancing overall operational efficiency.

2.7. Improved Accountability and Transparency

The Single Window System (SWS) has significantly minimized, and in certain instances eradicated, direct human interactions between officials in governmental trade facilitation agencies and the private sector. Traders and associated stakeholders now benefit from automated system notifications that provide real-time updates on the progress of their application approvals, simplifying the tracking process. This enhanced transparency allows stakeholders to monitor the time taken by various entities and government agencies to process documents across multiple stages. Such visibility has positively influenced the accountability and responsiveness of these agencies, while concurrently diminishing opportunities for rent-seeking behaviors (Kapidani et al., 2021).

"The SWS has made it more secure to facilitate trade since government officers no longer need to handle a lot of money."

CHAPTER 3:

THE IVORIAN SWS: GUICHET UNIQUE DU COMMERCE EXTÉRIEUR (GUCE)

This chapter provides an in-depth analysis of the Single Window System (SWS) in Côte d'Ivoire, with a specific focus on its implementation at the Port of Abidjan. It begins with an overview of the port, highlighting its strategic role in regional trade and economic development. We then examine the current status and progress of the Ivorian SWS, assessing its achievements and ongoing challenges.

A comparative analysis with the UN's Evolutionary Model for SWS implementation offers valuable insights into how the Ivorian system aligns with global best practices. Additionally, we explore the governance structure of the Ivorian SWS, identifying key stakeholders and their roles in its development and operationalization.

Furthermore, this chapter outlines the critical factors influencing SWS implementation success in the West African context using the Port of Abidjan as a case study.

3.1. Overview of the Abidjan Port

Côte D'Ivoire has the largest economy in francophone Sub-Saharan Africa and the third largest in West Africa, with a population of 26.3 million and a GDP of $61.502 billion (Dutta & Lanvin, 2020). The Ivorian economy is heavily dependent on the maritime industry, particularly the port of Abidjan, for exporting and importing essential materials that are vital for agricultural production, machinery, and other consumption needs.

In 2023, the Port of Abidjan experienced a significant increase in container traffic, handling approximately 1.23 million twenty-foot equivalent units (TEUs), which represents a 46% rise compared to the previous year. This surge is largely attributed to the operationalization of the port's second container terminal (TC2), which has enhanced its capacity to accommodate larger vessels and increased cargo volumes.

Additionally, the port's overall freight traffic grew by 21%, reaching 34.8 million tonnes in 2023, up from 28.6 million tonnes in 2022.

These developments underscore the Port of Abidjan's expanding role as a pivotal maritime hub in West Africa. The port handles 80% of the country's maritime traffic and ranks second in freight volume among the 25 ports along the West African coast, after Nigeria's Lekki Deep Sea Port. This prominence is partly due to its role as a gateway for the landlocked countries of Burkina Faso, Mali, and Niger (PAA, 2020).

In response, the Ivorian government introduced the Single Window System (SWS) at the Port of Abidjan in 2013 to facilitate trade and enhance port competitiveness. Despite its benefits, implementing the SWS is a complex and costly endeavor that demands significant effort, financial investment, a shift in mindset, and, most importantly, political will from the Ivorian government.

As SWS is relatively new and sparsely researched in Côte d'Ivoire, there is currently no study on the critical factors influencing its implementation at the Port of Abidjan.

3.2. Current Status and Progress of the Ivorian SWS

Drawing from official documents provided by the implementing company, GUCE-CI, **Table 3** presents a detailed snapshot of the progress made in deploying the 19 key modules designed to achieve a fully paperless Single Window System (SWS) at the Port of Abidjan. These modules serve as the backbone of the digital transformation, enabling seamless interaction among multiple stakeholders through the SWS platform. Each module represents a critical piece of the larger vision of an interconnected, efficient, and entirely dematerialized port ecosystem.

Table 3. Implementation status of the Ivorian SWS

	Ivorian SWS Modules					
	Modules	Fully paperless	Not fully paperless	Developed or being developed not in use	Not developed	Main stakeholder
1	e-forex	✓				(Commercial bank) / (Importers & Exporters)

2	e-license	✓				(Ministry of Trade) / (Ministry of Agriculture)
3	e-manifest	✓				(PAA) / (Shipping agent) / (Customs)/ (DGAMP)
4	e-movement				✓	(Stevedore Company) / (PAA)
5	e-payment			✓		All stakeholders
6	e-phytosanitary		✓			(Ministry of Agriculture)
7	e-risk	✓				(Customs)
8	e-sad / DAU		✓			(Customs)
9	e-transhipment			✓		(Stevedore Company) / (Customs)
10	e-voyage	✓				(PAA) / (Shipping Agent)
11	Collaborative e-visit			✓		(Customs)
12	Exemption			✓		(Customs)
13	Insurance Certificate	✓				(Insurance company)
14	Certificate Of Origin			✓		(Importers & Exporters) / (Customs)

15	Timbe r			✓		(Importers & Exporters)
16	Reque st for value certific ate	✓				(Customs) / (Importers & Exporters)
17	Certifi cate of confor mity	✓				(Importers & Exporters)
18	Trade transa ction	✓				(Importers & Exporters)
19	Integr al Bsc	✓				(DGAMP)

Source: GUCE-CI (2021)

Since its official launch in 2013, the journey toward a fully digitalized Single Window System (SWS) at the port of Abidjan has been a long and intricate process. Over the span of seven years, significant progress has been made, yet challenges remain.

An in-depth analysis of stakeholder documents has pro-vided valuable insights into this transformation. The data reveals that the implementing company has identified 19 key modules essential to achieving complete demterial-ization. Among them, 10 modules have already transi-tioned to a fully paperless system, while 2 still rely on partial paper-based processes. Meanwhile, 6 modules are either in development or awaiting implementation, and one module remains entirely undeveloped.

Beyond the technical aspects, the data also sheds light on the various stakeholders involved, each playing a crucial role in this digital shift. The findings underscore the complexity of the initiative, highlighting both achievements and the hurdles that must still be overcome to realize a seamless, fully digital port system.

Documents from Guce-ci confirm the following:

"The initial contract signed between the State of Côte D'Ivoire and Webb Fontaine gave the implementing company a period of five years to implement a completely dematerialized SWS in the port of Abidjan." (GUCE-CI, 2021).

Despite ambitious planning, the deadline ultimately slipped beyond reach. A mix of unforeseen challenges and operational hurdles contributed to the delay. During PowerPoint presentations, officials from the implementing company candidly outlined the obstacles they faced setbacks that slowed progress and complicated the path forward.

3.3. A Comparative Analysis of the Ivorian SWS with the UN's Evolutionary Model

This section begins by comparing Côte d'Ivoire's Single Window System (SWS) to the Evolutionary Development Model of Single Window, highlighting key similarities and differences. It then examines the implementation process, mapping out the current stage of completion at each level of development, providing a clear picture of progress and remaining challenges.

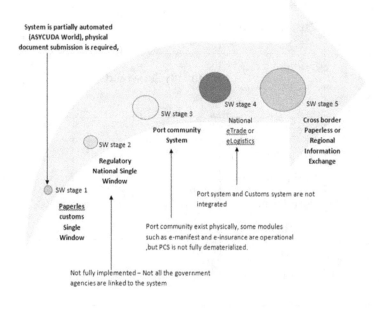

Figure 1. Comparison of the Ivorian SWS with the "Evolutionary Development Model of Single Window"

Table 4. Comparison of the Ivorian SWS with the "Evolutionary Development Model of Single Window"

Levels / Stages	A Single Window Roadmap in Five Evolutionary Stages (UNECE 2011)	The Ivorian SWS	Percentage of completion
Stage 1	Paperless Customs	Not fully implemented	90%
	e-Payment for Customs Duty	Fully implemented	100%
	Container Loading List	Fully implemented	100%
	Simple e-Documents Exchange with Port Authority and/or Terminal Operators	Not fully implemented	50%

Level 2	Connecting Other Government Backend IT systems,	Not fully implemented/ Partially manual	50%
	e-Permit Exchange with Paperless Customs System	Not fully implemented/ Partially manual	50%
Level 3	e-Documents Exchange stakeholders within the (air, sea, dry) port community	Not fully implemented (Only implemented for Ships Agent & Terminal Operators.)	30%
Level 4	An integrated national logistics platform with also traders and logistics service providers information exchange	Traders, Some Banks & Freight Forwarders are connected to the SWS. However, the Port of Abidjan systems is not integrated into the SWS platform.	40%

	A regional information exchange system	Not implemented	10%
Level 5			

Source: GUCE-CI (2021)

Implementing a Single Window System (SWS) remains a formidable challenge for many developing countries, including Côte d'Ivoire (Peterson, 2017). In Côte d'Ivoire, the journey toward a fully digitalized trade facilitation system began in 2013. Yet, even after seven years, the country has not fully realized its ultimate goal: complete dematerialization of import and export operations through the Port of Abidjan, an essential hub handling 90% of the nation's foreign trade.

Understanding this ongoing struggle provides crucial insights into the complexities of SWS implementation in developing economies. Research in this field, particularly in the Ivorian context, has consistently highlighted the need for strategies that enhance stakeholder engagement, deepen understanding of critical success factors, and address persistent barriers to adoption. At its core, this study seeks to bridge that gap, offering practical solutions to drive meaningful progress.

3.4. Governance of the Ivorian SWS

A significant success factor in the implementation of a Single Window is the governance aspect, which combines a number of strategic elements (Torlak et al., 2020). In the port of Abidjan, the Build-Operate-Transfer (BOT) approach of the Public Private Partnership business model is being used for the implementation of SWS. This approach to describing PPP for the SWS project captures legal ownership and control of the project assets (Delmon, 2015). Under the SWS BOT project, the private company owns the project assets until they are transferred at the end of the contract to the government or public agency. Currently, the Ivorian government holds 70% of the shares while a private partner (Web-Fontaine) holds 30% (GUCE-CI, 2021) with the end goal that all of Web-Fontaine shares will be transferred to the government at the end of the contract duration. In terms of governance, the SWS project in the port is overseen by the Ministry of Commerce as the lead agency (GUCE-CI, 2021).

In line with the above BOT approach, the Ivorian government has chosen the Ministry of Commerce as the lead agency because it finds it more representative and able to federate all the stakeholders involved in foreign trade (GUCE-CI, 2021). This approach of the Ivorian government is contrary to the proposal of Wang (2016), who suggests customs as the best lead agency for a successful implementation of SWS in the port.

The importance of the choice of lead agency comes from the fact that to be able to provide adequate services accessible to all stakeholders, the pool of the Single Window governing body should include all stakeholders in the Foreign Trade community (all public and private entities concerned by the Single Window) (Jovic et al., 2021). As a result, the supreme governing body of the entity in charge of the Single Window should be representative of the whole Foreign Trade chain, notably in the case of a PPP model, so as to avoid interest being oriented towards a single organization. In other words, the relevance of the services provided by the Single Window depends on the integration and involvement of the partners - public and private - in Foreign Trade, hence the importance of choosing an effective lead agency (Wang, 2016).

3.5. Key Stakeholders and Development Stage of the Ivorian SWS

Port community members include port facility and infrastructure providers, cargo handling service providers, shipping operators and agents, land transport operators, and cargo representatives (Jovic et al., 2021). Port activity traditionally involves several private and public organizations that operate fragmentedly (Caldeirinha et al.,2022). Interviews with various stakeholders revealed that the Ivorian SWS is inspired by the UN guidelines, which decompose the implementation of the SWS into five stages.

According to the UNECE (2013) SWS implementation roadmap, the foundation of a Single Window System should begin with a fully paperless customs platform. In Côte d'Ivoire, this initial stage is anchored in ASYCUDA World, the country's customs IT system. However, despite its automation capabilities, the system remains only partially digital, as physical documents are still required at various stages of the clearance process, which highlights a key hurdle in the transition toward full dematerialization.

At this stage, the implementing company partnered with Ivorian Customs to digitize the first set of modules, including RFCV, aimed at streamlining the pre-clearance of goods. In an effort to accelerate the transition, the company assumed control over several key customs functions to integrate them into the digital system. However, this shift proved challenging for Customs authorities, as it raised concerns about operational control and the adaptation to new digital workflows.

"In addition, we did not like the fact that the development of certain customs modules (RFCV, EDAU, etc.) be entrusted to an external structure. The Customs saw in this its prerogatives being withdrawn, and high risk of its data being misused."

The journey toward a fully digital Single Window System (SWS) follows a structured roadmap, with each stage bringing new challenges and key stakeholders into the process.

At the initial stage, Customs plays the central role in dematerialization, as it forms the backbone of trade facilitation. The UNECE (2013) roadmap specifies that this phase should establish a paperless customs system, ensuring a seamless transition away from physical documentation.

Progressing to the second stage, integration extends beyond Customs to Government Back-end IT systems, such as E-Permit Exchanges and Paperless Customs Systems. In Côte d'Ivoire, this phase is partially implemented, involving critical institutions such as the Maritime Affairs Administration, the Ministry of Commerce, and the Ministry of Agriculture, each of which plays a crucial role in regulatory oversight and trade governance.

The third stage marks a significant shift towards e-document exchanges among stakeholders within the broader port community, which includes air, sea, and dry ports. In Côte d'Ivoire, this transition is underway, supported by the implementation of a Port Community System (PCS) featuring modules such as E-Manifest, E-Voyage, and E-Movement. At this stage, key players include the Port Authority of Abidjan (PAA), shipping companies, stevedores, and insurance firms. However, interviews with stakeholders reveal that despite efforts by the implementing company, post-clearance operations remain largely manual, underscoring the need for further digital transformation.

The final frontier, the fifth stage, envisions cross-border paperless trade, where regional trade partners seamlessly exchange digital documentation. Côte d'Ivoire and Senegal took an early step in this direction, piloting the electronic transmission of Certificates of Origin as early as 2004. However, legal and technical roadblocks hindered progress, bringing the experiment to a standstill. A major barrier remains: Côte d'Ivoire has yet to pass legislation recognizing electronic documents and signatures, a critical requirement for a regional Single Window System. Until this legal framework is established, the vision of a fully integrated, paperless trade corridor across West Africa remains out of reach.

"As an implementing company, today...I can say that just more than 50% of our goals are achieved. Many modules are operational, some are not, and some modules are yet to be conceived. We have made a lot of progress, but we have not yet achieved the stage of a full paperless SWS intended."

According to participants, the dematerialization of all pre-clearance processes has been fully achieved.

However, when it comes to clearance and post-clearance operations, significant progress has been made, yet gaps remain in achieving a completely paperless system. Figure 1 provides a comparative analysis of Côte d'Ivoire's Single Window System (SWS) against the UNECE (2013) roadmap, based on data sourced from official documents provided by the implementing company.

To gain deeper insights into the implementation process, this research conducted interviews with fourteen participants, each representing a different public or private organization involved in the SWS deployment at the Port of Abidjan. These stakeholders encompass a broad spectrum of entities: on one side, private sector players such as shipping agents, stevedoring companies, clearing agents, and insurance firms; on the other, government agencies, including Customs and the Port Authority.

Yet, amid this diverse network, interviews revealed that two key stakeholders stand out as the principal drivers of the SWS implementation. As one participant put it:

The implementation of the SWS at the Port of Abidjan is primarily influenced by two key actors: the Customs and the Port Authorities. Customs, as a state public service, are responsible for implementing and enforcing the regulatory provisions governing the movement of people, goods, means of transport, and capital. The Port Authorities (PAA) play a key role in coordinating the activities of all stakeholders within the port community system.

"The frank collaboration between The Customs and the Port Authorities (PAA) is a prerequisite in establishing an effective Single Window System because the removal of goods must pass through green lights given by the Customs."

The Port Authority of Abidjan (PAA) plays a pivotal role as both the architect and coordinator of the port's development strategy, overseeing the seamless operation of the entire Port Community. Entrusted with ensuring the seaport's safety, sustainability, and competitiveness, the PAA stands as a cornerstone in the successful implementation of the Single Window System (SWS).

Beyond its regulatory function, the SWS presents an opportunity for the PAA to evolve into a true digital hub and neutral data manager, optimizing the transport and logistics chain. By gathering and exchanging real-time information among various stakeholders, the system has the potential to streamline logistics, enhance operational efficiency, and maximize the use of transport infrastructure.

Within this ecosystem, the client structure is shaped by key players. Shipping lines and freight forwarders hold the most influential roles, followed by importers, exporters, and shipping agents, each contributing to the intricate network that drives port operations.

3.6 Factors Key to SWS Implementation in West African Countries Context: Case of the Port of Abidjan

The Single Window System (SWS) is key to modernizing port operations by streamlining trade procedures, enhancing regulatory compliance, and reducing transaction costs. While widely adopted in developed economies, its implementation in West African ports presents unique challenges and opportunities.

This section examines the critical factors influencing SWS deployment in West Africa, focusing on the Port of Abidjan as a key regional trade hub. It explores enablers such as political will, technology, inter-agency coordination, legal frameworks, and stakeholder engagement, along-side potential barriers.

By analyzing Abidjan's experience, this research provides insights for policymakers and trade stakeholders, high-lighting essential steps to enhance port efficiency and competitiveness in the region.

3.6.1. Lack of Strong Political Will

The implementation of the Single Window System (SWS) has encountered significant challenges due to a lack of ro-bust political will. This deficiency is evident in the reluc-tance of certain managerial figures to embrace the SWS, necessitating decisive political intervention to enlist piv-otal entities such as the Port Authority of Abidjan and Customs into the initiative. Throughout the various phases of deployment, this factor has been identified as critical, apart from the second stage, where public stake-holders more reliant on governmental directives are in-volved. Interviews have revealed that this absence of strong political commitment has led to delays in the SWS's rollout. Document analysis corroborates these findings, indicating that even eight years after its inception, the SWS at the Port of Abidjan has yet to achieve its objective of a fully paperless system.

3.6.2. Inadequate Legal Framework

"Inadequate legal framework" is one of the two factors that have a high level of congruence (five out of fourteen) among the stakeholders and across all the stages of implementation except the second stage. The five stakeholders for whom the criticality level is high include the following: Customs, the Importer/Exporter, the Clearing and Forwarding Agent, GUCE-CI, and the shipping agent. This is explained by the fact that, despite the laws put in place at the early stage of the implementation, some key laws on electronic signature are missing, which prevent a full dematerialization of the SWS. In other words, the current legal framework in place in Côte D'Ivoire is not sufficient to achieve a full paperless SWS. This was also confirmed from the analysis of documents.

Even though the factors "Inadequate Legal framework" and "Lack of strong political will" have achieved the same congruence, "Inadequate Legal framework" comes after because it emerges from the exchanges with participants that by the action of political will, the government at the beginning of the implementation system in 2014 enacted new laws to legalize the digitalization of import and export procedures to facilitate the SWS implementation. Unfortunately, these laws did not take into consideration all the requirements of digitalization in trade, such as electronic signatures. Thus, hampering the smooth operationalization at some stages of the implementation process (Kabui et al. 2019).

The implementation of the Single Window System (SWS) in Côte d'Ivoire has faced significant challenges due to an inadequate legal framework. Despite the introduction of new laws in 2014 to support the digitalization of import and export procedures, essential legislation, such as those governing electronic signatures, were overlooked. This oversight has prevented the SWS from achieving a fully paperless operation, as certain digital processes lack legal recognition. Consequently, stakeholders, including importers, exporters, clearing and forwarding agents, and shipping agents, have experienced delays and inefficiencies. Interviews and document analyses confirm that, even after eight years, SWS has not met its goal of complete digitalization, primarily due to these legal shortcomings. While both "Inadequate Legal Frame-work" and "Lack of Strong Political Will" have been identified as critical issues, the former is particularly impactful because, despite initial political efforts to enact supportive laws, the failure to address all necessary aspects of digital trade such as electronic signatures has hindered smooth implementation at various stages.

3.6.3. Inadequate ICT Infrastructure

The introduction of the Single Window System (SWS) in Côte d'Ivoire has faced significant hurdles due to insufficient information and communication technology (ICT) infrastructure. Key stakeholders, including the Port Authority of Abidjan, importers, exporters, clearing and forwarding agents, and the company responsible for implementing the system, have been particularly affected. These challenges stem from a lack of computer skills, unpreparedness for digital operations, system malfunctions, incompatibility between the SWS and existing systems of major stakeholders like the Port Authority, and unstable internet connections. As a result, many organizations struggle with a shortage of qualified staff and adequate technological resources to effectively utilize the new system. These issues have been consistently high-lighted in various reports and analyses.

3.6.4. Lack of Top Management Support

The introduction of the Single Window System (SWS) in Côte d'Ivoire faced significant delays due to a lack of support from top management in key organizations. Notably, leaders within the Port Authority of Abidjan and two other major entities, which play crucial roles in the country's import and export activities, were initially resistant to adopting the SWS. This resistance stemmed from their focus on developing their own internal digital systems and reluctance to integrate with the new centralized platform. Consequently, the implementation of the SWS was postponed within these organizations. As of 2021, eight years after its initial launch, the SWS at the Port of Abidjan had yet to achieve its goal of a completely paperless system.

3.6.5. Resistance to Change from Personnel

The implementation of the Single Window System (SWS) in Côte d'Ivoire encountered significant obstacles due to resistance from personnel within key organizations, notably clearing and forwarding agents, as well as major public entities such as the Port Authority of Abidjan and Customs. Many employees, accustomed to traditional practices like physical document inspections and face-to-face client interactions, were hesitant to adopt the new digital system. This reluctance led to delays in the SWS rollout. In certain cases, opposition intensified, resulting in the dismissal of two IT directors from Customs due to their resistance. There were also isolated incidents where vehicles belonging to the implementation team's personnel were attacked. These actions were primarily driven by workers' fears of job loss stemming from the new system.

3.6.6. Lack of Partnership and Collaboration Among Stakeholders

The implementation of the Single Window System (SWS) in Côte d'Ivoire faced significant challenges due to a lack of collaboration among key stakeholders. The company responsible for implementing the system encountered considerable difficulties in connecting certain parties to the SWS. Some managers were reluctant to fully digitize their operations, leading to a lack of cooperation with the implementation team. This reluctance hindered the project's progress and made it challenging for the implementing company to adhere to the planned schedule.

3.6.7. Fear of Security and Privacy

The introduction of the Single Window System (SWS) in Côte d'Ivoire encountered significant challenges due to concerns over data security and privacy. The Port Authority of Abidjan (PAA) was particularly apprehensive about the potential for sensitive information shared on the SWS platform to be hacked and misused by competitors. This fear led to delays in the system's implementation, as the PAA hesitated to fully embrace the digital platform without assurances regarding the protection of their data.

This situation underscores the critical importance of robust security measures and clear privacy policies when introducing digital systems in sensitive sectors. Addressing these concerns is essential to gain the trust of all stakeholders and ensure the successful adoption of technological advancements.

3.6.8. Political Instability

Political instability is a critical factor that can significantly disrupt the implementation of the Single Window System (SWS) in Côte d'Ivoire. While it is a rare occurrence, when political instability does arise, it affects all stakeholders simultaneously, leading to delays, work stoppages, and, in severe cases, the permanent closure of companies.

For instance, during the 2010-2011 post-election crisis in Côte d'Ivoire, political instability caused severe disruptions in the transport and logistics sector, leading to increased costs, delays, and risks for traders.

Similarly, in 2019, political unrest in Chile resulted in violent protests, roadblocks, and vandalism that affected the operations of ports, airports, and customs offices. These examples demonstrate that political instability can have a significant negative impact on trade facilitation performance.

The unpredictability of political instability underscores the need for flexible and adaptable systems that can withstand sudden disruptions. Although instances of political instability are infrequent, their impact on importers, exporters, and the wider trading community can be devastating. Therefore, addressing this issue is essential to ensure the resilience and effectiveness of the Single Window System in the face of such events.

Tackling this issue requires a nuanced approach, acknowledging the vulnerability of the system to external geopolitical factors and preparing contingency plans to mitigate the consequences of political instability. This highlights that the success of the SWS depends not only on overcoming daily challenges but also on being prepared for exceptional events that can shake the foundations of international trade.

3.6.9. Lead Agency's Lack of Clarity and Inclusion

In the implementation of the Single Window System (SWS) in Côte d'Ivoire, the role of the lead agency was pivotal. The organization chosen to oversee the project (Ministry of Trade), received broad support from stakeholders. Initially, some stakeholders had concerns about the clarity and inclusiveness of the implementing company's approach. However, these issues were promptly addressed and did not cause significant delays. Consequently, the lead agency's clarity and inclusiveness were not major obstacles to the SWS implementation in the port of Abidjan. This outcome contrasts with recommendations from other studies, such as Wang (2016), which suggested that customs should be the lead agency in SWS implementation. In the case of the port of Abidjan, the Ministry of Trade was well-received by stakeholders.

3.6.10. Lack of Financial Resources

In the implementation of the Single Window System (SWS) in Abidjan, the lack of financial resources was identified as a critical factor. However, this issue did not significantly hinder the process. This was largely due to the Public-Private Partnership (PPP) model adopted by the government, which facilitated the sharing of costs between the public and private sectors. As a result, expenses related to training and acquiring necessary technology were managed without causing delays or interruptions in the SWS implementation.

CHAPTER 4:

THE EVOLUTION OF SINGLE WINDOW IMPLEMENTATION IN WEST AFRICA: A COMPARATIVE ANALYSIS

The evolution of the Single Window System (SWS) in West Africa represents a transformative step toward enhancing trade efficiency, economic integration, and regional competitiveness. This chapter provides a comparative analysis of SWS implementation across various countries, using the UNECE Model (2011) as a benchmark to assess progress through five evolutionary stages ranging from basic digital customs operations to a fully integrated regional information-sharing system. By exploring each stage, from paperless customs processing to cross-border interoperability, this chapter highlights key success factors such as technological readiness, stakeholder engagement, government commitment, and policy harmonization, offering valuable insights into the region's digital trade transformation.

4.1. Level 1 The Dawn of Paperless Customs Processes

At the foundational stage, countries are expected to transition from traditional, paper-heavy customs operations to a streamlined, digital framework. Côte d'Ivoire (GUCE-CI), Senegal (ORBUS), Guinea (GUCE-G), and Ghana (UNIPASS) have made substantial progress, with most processes either in operation or underway. However, Gambia and Sierra Leone lag behind, showing no implementation of Level 1 features.

A crucial observation at this stage is the efficacy of the Container Loading List. While Côte d'Ivoire, Guinea, Ghana, and Cape Verde have successfully implemented this function, Senegal still struggles with inefficiencies. Nevertheless, all operational countries have established an effective electronic interchange of documents with the

Port Authority, setting the foundation for future advancements.

4.2. Level 2 Bridging Public Stakeholders and Certificate Exchange

The second level marks the integration of public stakeholders into the Single Window system, fostering connectivity and seamless exchange of certificates within customs frameworks. Côte d'Ivoire, Senegal, Guinea, Ghana, and Cape Verde lead in this domain, boasting fully operational stakeholder connections.

Yet, challenges persist. Guinea and Cape Verde have yet to achieve full digital exchange of certificates, with processes still in development. Meanwhile, Gambia and Sierra Leone remain completely inactive, underscoring the disparities in regional implementation.

4.3. Level 3 Towards a Paperless Port Community

This level introduces digital exchanges among port stakeholders, enhancing collaboration and operational efficiency. Ghana has demonstrated commendable progress, actively working towards deployment, while Côte d'Ivoire is also making strides in its implementation.

Conversely, Senegal possesses the necessary technological framework but has not yet deployed it, highlighting a gap between infrastructure readiness and execution. Guinea, Cape Verde, Gambia, and Sierra Leone have yet to embark on this phase, indicating a significant roadblock in regional digitization efforts.

4.4. Level 4 Establishing a National Logistics Platform

A fully integrated logistics platform is critical for harmonizing trade operations across different actors, from merchants to service providers. Côte d'Ivoire and Ghana are actively developing their logistics frameworks to ensure seamless information exchange.

Despite having a viable solution, Senegal has not yet moved to full deployment. Meanwhile, Guinea, Cape Verde, Gambia, and Sierra Leone have made no notable progress at this level, further delaying the realization of an interconnected trade ecosystem.

4.5. Level 5 The Pinnacle: Regional Information Sharing System

At the highest level, a regional information-sharing system fosters interoperability between national Single Windows, boosting efficiency across borders. Côte d'Ivoire and Senegal stand as pioneers, having successfully completed the Pilot E-CO project in 2014.

Guinea, Ghana, and Cape Verde are making gradual advancements, with implementation plans "in the pipeline." However, Gambia and Sierra Leone remain absent from these discussions, illustrating a stark contrast in regional integration efforts.

4.6. General Observations and Country Ranking

Table 5. Ranking of West African SWS implementation status

Rank	Country	Implementation Status
1st	Côte d'Ivoire	The most advanced, with multiple levels effectively operational and a completed Pilot E-CO project.
2nd	Senegal	Strong framework but faces deployment challenges at Levels 3 & 4.

3rd	Ghana	Solid implementation in Levels 1 & 2; still working on Levels 3-5.
4th	Guinea	Slightly behind Ghana but showing commitment to progress.
5th	Cape Verde	Moderate advancements, particularly in foundational levels.
6th	Gambia	Minimal implementation beyond Level 1.
7th	Sierra Leone	No visible implementation to date.

The implementation of the Single Window System across West Africa reveals a clear divide between leading countries and those yet to embark on the journey. Côte d'Ivoire and Senegal stand at the forefront, having successfully integrated multiple levels and established themselves as regional benchmarks. Ghana and Guinea follow closely, with ongoing efforts to refine their systems. Cape Verde remains in a transitional phase, whereas Gambia and Sierra Leone require urgent intervention to initiate their digital transformation.

For West Africa to fully harness the benefits of an interconnected trade system, regional cooperation, investment in digital solutions, and policy alignment with international best practices will be indispensable. With strategic interventions, the Single Window System can revolutionize trade operations, driving economic growth and strengthening the region's position in global commerce.

Table 6. Comparison of Single Windows in Some Countries

Comparative Study of the Implementation of the Single Window for External Trade (GUCE) with the UNECE Model (2011)

Levels / Steps	A roadmap for Single Windows in five evolutionary steps (UNECE 2011)	GUCE -CI IVORY COAST	ORBUS and ORBUS LOGISTICS SENEGAL	GUCE-G GUINEA	UNIPASS GHANA	JUP (Cape Verde)	Gambia	Sierra Leone
Level 1	Paperless customs clearance	Underway	Underway	Underway	Underway	N/A	N/A	N/A
	Electronic payment of customs duties	Underway	Underway	Underway	Underway	Underway	N/A	N/A
	Container Loading List	Effective	Ineffective	Effective	Effective	Effective	N/A	N/A
	Electronic interchange of documents with the Port Authority.	Effective	Effective	Effective	Effective	Effective	N/A	N/A
Level 2	Connecting public stakeholders to the Single Window.	Effective	Effective	Effective	Effective	Effective	N/A	N/A
Level 3	Paperless exchange of certificates with the customs system.	Effective	Effective	Underway	Effective	Underway	N/A	N/A
	Paperless exchange between stakeholders in the port community.	Underway	Existing solution deployed	N/A	Underway	N/A	N/A	N/A
Level 4	An integrated national logistics platform that enables information exchange with merchants and logistics service providers.	Underway	Existing solution not deployed	N/A	Underway	N/A	N/A	N/A
Level 5	A regional information sharing system	In the pipeline (Pilot E-CO Completed in 2014)	In the pipeline (Pilot E-CO Completed in 2014)	In the pipeline	In the pipeline	In the pipeline	N/A	N/A

NB: The table below compares the current situation in 2021 of some countries according to the UNECE model

CHAPTER 5:

LESSONS LEARNED FROM THE IVORIAN SWS AND APPLICATION TO OTHER DEVELOPING COUNTRIES

The implementation of a Single Window System (SWS) is a transformative step toward enhancing trade efficiency and port competitiveness, particularly in developing countries. This chapter draws from the Ivorian experience to highlight key lessons and best practices that can be adapted to similar contexts worldwide.

The chapter first examines the practical contributions of this research, offering insights into how port authorities, government agencies, and private sector stakeholders can overcome challenges and optimize SWS implementation. It explores the role of government support, regulatory frameworks, stakeholder engagement, and digital infrastructure in ensuring a successful rollout.

Furthermore, the chapter discusses transferable lessons from the Port of Abidjan, emphasizing the importance of political commitment, legal reforms, technological investment, and change management. It underscores the need for customized approaches based on each country's unique socio-economic conditions, ensuring that SWS implementation is both efficient and sustainable.

By analyzing the successes and obstacles faced in Côte d'Ivoire, this chapter serves as a strategic guide for other developing nations, providing actionable recommendations to streamline trade processes and drive economic growth.

5.1. Contribution to Practice

This study also contributes to managerial practice based on the findings of this research. Given the relevance of SWS for port competitiveness and trade facilitation (Kabui et al., 2019), this study's conclusions provide the opportunity to offer the participating stakeholders and probably other West African ports transferable relevant information that can be utilized to facilitate SWS in their ports (Tracy, 2000). The transferability of this research may be enhanced by the fact that most West African ports have the same private operators (Bollore, MSC, Maersk Line) (IPCOEA, 2021). Thus, the same working methods are found at these ports. Additionally, these countries meet most of the political, economic, social, and environmental conditions of Côte d'Ivoire (World Bank, 2020).

Unlike previous studies on SWS, this study extends our understanding further by evaluating the criticality of factors and by mapping the critical factors of SWS with key stakeholders at every implementation stage. This would enable decision-makers to determine which factors are critical for each key stakeholder at every implementation stage of the SWS. Thus, allowing the prioritization of decision makers' actions to minimize the impact of challenges in the implementation process of SWS.

The contribution to practice is especially relevant today since businesses operate in increasingly changing environments (Dutta & Lanvin, 2020), mainly following the

COVID-19 pandemic that has prompted the need for digitalization (IPCOEA, 2021). The following is a summary of recommendations made to this study's participants and possibly other developing country ports:

Firstly, based on the findings of this study, the success of developing countries' SWS would largely depend on government support and available resources. In other words, the Government has a crucial role to play, particularly in areas of legislation and regulations to control SWS activities (Joshi, 2016). Funding should be made available to improve ICT infrastructure, education, and training of public and private stakeholders' personnel.

Secondly, considering the challenges of mobilizing support from the stakeholders, using an "Idea Champion" approach is recommended. An "idea champion" approach rests on one highly respected person who can coordinate and overcome obstacles by leveraging close personal ties and pursuing informal avenues of influence. This person could be the president of the country or the Prime Minister. This solution worked in the republic of Benin, where the "idea champion" is the country's president. Also, in Ghana, it helped advance the port's SWS implementation, with the Vice-President being the "idea champion" (IPCOEA, 2021).

Thirdly, developing countries would benefit from establishing an independent monitoring and evaluation body, supported by the government but independent in its operation and structure. This would help monitor SWS projects closely and ensure transparency or expose any corruption (Caldeirinha et al., 2022).

Lastly, the public and private stakeholders need to attract, retain, and develop staff with skills and competencies in business process analysis, project management, and IT areas, which are crucial for the sustainability of the Single Window System (Aryee & Hansen, 2022).

5.2. Lessons Learned and Applications to Other Developing Countries

This research provides several key lessons that can be applied to other developing countries seeking to implement a Single Window System (SWS) in their ports. While the case study focused specifically on the port of Abidjan in Côte d'Ivoire, many other developing countries face similar challenges that must be addressed for successful SWS implementation.

One of the most important lessons is the need for strong government support and commitment throughout the implementation process. As was evident in the case of Côte d'Ivoire, "lack of strong political will" was one of the main factors hindering the full rollout of the SWS. Without high-level political backing to both encourage and compel stakeholder participation and cooperation, progress will be slow.

Other developing countries can apply this lesson by ensuring the highest level of political endorsement of the SWS project from the upper echelons of government (the office of the presidency). An "idea champion" approach where the head of state takes personal responsibility for the initiative can help overcome obstacles (GUCE-CI, 2021). Government commitment must also translate into the allocation of sufficient financial resources and willingness to modify laws and regulations as needed.

An adequate legal framework is essential for implementing a paperless SWS, yet this was lacking in Côte d'Ivoire. Developing countries must assess existing laws and be prepared to enact new legislation covering areas like electronic signatures, data privacy, cybersecurity, and e-transactions. Laws may also be needed to mandate the use of the SWS by traders and participating government agencies. The exact legal regulations will differ based on each country's starting point or may be adapted to reflect each country's circumstances and progress. However, this study asserts that the political will to craft a comprehensive legal framework should be secured upfront rather than later when the implementation process is in motion. This can be coupled with stakeholder consultations to help determine high-priority areas for legal reform.

While Côte d'Ivoire had basic ICT in place, inadequate infrastructure posed a major barrier. Unstable internet connectivity, limited internet data bandwidth, and overall computer illiteracy of the working populace hampered the SWS rollout. Developing countries must devote resources to upgrading ICT infrastructure and networks to support an electronic SWS. Governments can assist by removing taxes on essential ICT imports and services needed for SWS implementation. Public access centers with computers and the internet can also help bridge the digital gap. Training programs should target both government personnel and private sector stakeholders to improve digital skills.

Resistance to change was another key factor uncovered in Côte d'Ivoire. Personnel from some public stakeholders opposed new digital processes that threatened traditional ways of working. Developing countries must employ change management strategies to secure buy-in at both organizational and individual levels, respectively. Change management plans can encompass training on new systems, demonstrating benefits, incentivizing usage, phased rollout, and addressing specific concerns. Leadership messaging and visioning are important to shift mindsets and cultures accustomed to paper processes. Change management is an ongoing process requiring dedicated resources and oversight.

The relative importance of different critical factors may vary based on each country's specific context. For example, landlocked developing countries highly dependent on neighboring seaports will prioritize regional interoperability with transit country SWS platforms. Small island nations with tourism-based economies may emphasize connectivity with airline systems. Post-conflict countries struggling with political instability may focus first on resilience and data backups.

While the broad factors identified in Côte d'Ivoire provide a useful starting checklist, countries should re-classify which ones are high, medium, or low priority based on their unique macro-environmental circumstances. This contextual reprioritization can help developing countries customize SWS implementation for maximum impact. Periodic re-evaluation of factors can also account for changing conditions over time.

Overall, developing countries can apply several insights and lessons from Côte d'Ivoire's experience in planning their own SWS initiatives. No two countries are identical, especially since each has its own ideology, and as such, adaptation is needed. Nevertheless, the key factors, implementation phases, stakeholder engagement strategies, change management techniques, and national-regional considerations can inform SWS rollout in developing country contexts worldwide. As more nations establish SWS platforms, knowledge sharing will be invaluable to accelerate trade growth and sustainable development.

CONCLUSION

This study explored the key factors influencing the adoption of the Single Window System (SWS) in developing countries, using the Port of Abidjan as a case study. Through in-depth interviews with fourteen key stakeholders, we gained valuable insights into the challenges and opportunities of SWS implementation.

Our research highlights that the impact of critical factors varies based on the stage of implementation and the stakeholders involved. Significant challenges identified include a lack of strong political will, an inadequate legal framework, insufficient ICT infrastructure, and limited top management support. These barriers are common in many developing countries and must be addressed to realize the full benefits of SWS.

Key Takeaways for Successful SWS Implementation

1. **Governments & Policy Makers:** Prioritizing investment in digital infrastructure, regulatory reforms, and interagency coordination will enhance transparency and efficiency in trade facilitation.

2. **Businesses & Traders:** Adopting automation, ensuring digital compliance, and integrating operations with SWS platforms will lead to smoother transactions and cost savings.

3. **Technology Providers:** Implementing emerging technologies like blockchain, artificial intelligence, and cloud computing can further optimize SWS, improving security, accuracy, and accessibility.

4. **International Cooperation:** Aligning trade policies and fostering cross-border collaboration will streamline trade processes and reduce inefficiencies.

Practical Steps for Moving Forward

- **User-Centered Design:** Future SWS developments should prioritize ease of use, accessibility, and seamless integration with existing business processes.

- **Ongoing Training & Capacity Building:** Regular

training for customs officers, traders, and service providers will ensure efficient adoption and use of the system.

- **Public-Private Partnerships:** Strong collaboration between governments, private sector stakeholders, and international organizations can drive system improvements and foster innovation.

- **Performance Monitoring & Feedback Loops:** Continuous evaluation and stakeholder feedback should guide enhancements to keep SWS effective and responsive to industry needs.

The Road Ahead

The Single Window System is not just a technological tool—it represents a fundamental shift in global trade operations. As more countries adopt and refine their systems, trade will become more digital, transparent, and interconnected. By fully embracing SWS, businesses and governments can unlock significant efficiencies, boost economic growth, and enhance global trade competitiveness.

Our study underscores the necessity of strong government support, an appropriate legal framework, and robust ICT infrastructure for successful SWS implementation. Additionally, Customs and Port Authorities must take a leading role in this process, given their central function in port operations and trade facilitation.

As the implementation of SWS at the Port of Abidjan is a relatively new initiative with limited prior research, this study provides valuable contributions to the field. While our findings are specific to Côte d'Ivoire, the insights gained can serve as a roadmap for other developing countries embarking on their own SWS journey. By learning from these experiences, nations can accelerate digital trade transformation and drive sustainable economic growth.

REFERENCES

1/ African Alliance for E-commerce. (2017). *Practical guide for Single Window system implementation* (Version 2). https://african-alliance.org/AACE/wpcontent/up-loads/2020/03/AACE-%E2%80%93-Guide-de-mise-en-%C5%93uvre-de-Guichets-Uniques-en-Afrique_VF-Mail.pdf.

2/ Aryee, J., and Hansen, A.S. (2022). De-politicization of digital systems for trade facilitation at the port of Tema: A soft systems methodology approach. *Case Studies on Transport Policy Open Access Volume 10, Issue 1, Pages 105 – 117.* 10.1016/j.cstp.2021.11.009

3/ Boblin, S. L., Ireland, S., Kirkpatrick, H., & Robertson, K. (2013). Using Stake's qualitative Case Study approach to explore the implementation of evidence-based practice. Qualitative Health Research, 23(9), 1267–1275

4/ Caldeirinha, V., Nabais, J.L., Pinto, C. (2022) Port Community Systems: Accelerating the Transition of

Seaports toward the Physical Internet — The Portuguese Case. Journal of Marine

5/ Delmon, J. (2015). Private sector investment in infrastructure: project finance, PPP projects and risk. New York, USA: Cambridge University Press

6/ Dutta, S., & Lanvin, B. (2020). The network readiness index 2020: accelerating digital transformation in a post-COVID global economy. Portulans Institute, WITSA: Washington, DC, USA. https://www.tralac.org/documents/resources/covid-19/4228-the-network-readiness-index-2020-accelerating-digital-transformation-post-covid-global-economy-portulansinstitute-october-2020/file.html

7/ Eriksson, P. and Kovalainen, A. (2015) Qualitative Methods in Business Research .2nd ed. London, Thousand Oaks, New Delhi, and Singapore: Sage.

8/ Gehman, J., Glaser, V.L., Eisenhardt, K.M., Gioia, D., Langley, A., and Corley, K.G. (2018) Finding Theory–Method Fit: A Comparison of Three Qualitative Approaches to Theory Building. Journal of Management Inquiry. 27(3), pp.284–300.

9/ Guichet Unique du Commerce Exterieur de Cote D'Ivoire (2021). Guichet unique pour le commerce exterieur. Portail transactionnel.
https://guce.gouv.ci/?namespaceController=home&lang=fr

10/ Improvement of Ports' Custom and Operations Efficiency in Africa (2020) Missions's reports. https://ip-coea.net/wpcontent/uploads/2021/03/Newsletter_Mar21_EN_Final.pdf

11/ Jović, M., Aksentijevic, S., Plentaj, B., Tijan, E. (2021) Port Community System Business Models. Conference: Digital Support from Crisis to Progressive Change. DOI: 10.18690/978-961-286-485-9.3

12/ Kabui, B. N., & Mwaura, T. G. D. P. (2019). Effect of Single Window System Procedures on Cargo Clearance Efficiency in Kenya: A Case for Mombasa Port. European Journal of Business and Management (Vol.11, No.24). file:///C:/Users/UP880550/Documents/Downloads/Chrome%20Downloads/49277-52916-1-PB%20(2).pdf

13/ Keretho, S. (2013). Evolving National Single Windows for Supply Chain Connectivity. In Asia Pacific Trade Facilitation Forum (Vol. 4, pp. 1-27). http://www.joebm.com/papers/302-BM00027.pdf

14/ Kivunja, C., & Kuyini, C, A. (2017) Understanding and Applying Research Paradigms in Educational Contexts. International Journal of Higher Education Vol 6, No 5. https://files.eric.ed.gov/fulltext/EJ1154775.pdf

15/ Moros-Daza, A., Amaya-Mier, R., García-Llinas, G., Voß, S. (2021) Port community system design for emerging economies: Case study Barranquilla, Colombia. Proceedings of the International Conference on Industrial Engineering and Operations Management, pp. 308–318. 978-179236125-8

16/ Piekkari and Welch, 2018; Piekkari, R., & Welch, C. (2018). The case study in management research: Beyond the positivist legacy of Eisenhardt and Yin? In C. Cassell, A. Cunliffe, & G. Grandy (Eds.), The SAGE handbook of qualitative business and management research methods (pp. 345–358). SAGE.

17/ Stake, R. E. (2006). Multiple case study analysis. Guilford Press.

18/ Tijan, E., Aksentijević, S., Ivanić, K., Jardas, M. (2019) Blockchain technology implementation in logistics. Sustainability (Switzerland) Open Access Volume 11, Issue 41, Article number 1185. DOI 10.3390/su11041185

19/ Torlak, I., Tijan, E., Aksentijević, S., Oblak, R. (2020). Analysis of port community system introduction in Croatian seaports - case study Split. Transactions on Maritime Science. Open AccessVolume 9, Issue 2, Pages 331 – 341. 10.7225/toms.v09.n02.015

20/ United Nations Economic Commission for Europe. (2013). Single window planning and implementation guide. https://unece.org/fileadmin/DAM/trade/Publications/ECE-TRADE-404_SingleWindow.pdf

21/ World Customs Organization. (2015). Annual report. http://www.wcoomd.org/-/media/wco/public/global/pdf/about-us/annual-reports/annual-report-2015_2016.pdf

22/ Wang, F. (2016). Interagency coordination in the implementation of single window: Lessons And good practice from Korea. World Customs Journal, 49.

https://worldcustomsjournal.org/Archives/Volume%2012%2C%20Number%201%20(Mar%202018)/1846%2001%20WCJ%20v12n1%20Feiyi.pdf

23/ Xenidis, Y., & Angelides, D. (2005). "The financial risks in build-operate-transfer projects," Construction Management and Economics, Taylor & Francis Journals, vol. 23(4), pages 431-441.

APPENDIX

Appendix 1: Key Stakeholders Interviewed and Involved in the Implementation of SWS at the Port of Abidjan

Organization	Position of Participant Interviewed	Role
Ministry of Commerce	Deputy Director of Trade	The Ministry of Commerce is responsible for the implementation and monitoring of the Government's policy on Trade and SMEs promotion. It handles the issue of certificates of origin. Also, it is the lead agency in the implementation of the SWS.
Ministry of Agriculture	Director of Plant Protection, Control and Quality	Cote D'Ivoire Plant Health Inspectorate Services controls the entry of seeds and plant material (phytosanitary) into Cote D'Ivoire to protect local agriculture. It also issues phytosanitary certificates for plant exports.
GUCE-CI	Business Analyst / Project Manager Port	It is the company that is implementing the Ivorian SWS.

	Community System (PCS)	
Ivoirian Office of Cargo Owners (OIC)	Director of Statistics	The Ivoirian Office of Cargo Owners (OIC) is, by definition, a council of cargo owners, i.e., an organization that represents and protects the interests of importers and exporters, transport services users, in connection with the transport of their goods.
Customs	IT System Manager	The Customs Department is responsible for the assessment, charge, and collection of customs and excise duties. It applies its stamp on certificates of origin issued by the Ministry of Commerce.
Directorate General of Maritime Affairs and Ports of Ivory Coast (DGAMP)	Director of IT Department	They ensure sustainable, safe, secure, clean, and efficient water transport for the benefit of stakeholders through effective regulation, coordination, and oversight of maritime affairs. They receive the Cargo Manifest sent by the Shipping Agent through the SWS.
Shipping Agent	Shipping Department Manager	The shipping agent acts as a representative of the owner of the ship and carries out all essential duties and obligations required by the ship's crew. He transmits the Cargo Manifest to the Port authorities, Maritime authorities, and Customs. He reports ships' arrival and departure to the port authorities.

Clearing & Forwarding Agents	Clearing & Forwarding Agent	The freight forwarder oversees the entire process of cargo movement, organizing the most suitable port schedules and negotiating the best rates available on the market.
Abidjan Ports Authority (PAA)	Expert in Port Information System	Abidjan Ports Authority (APA) acts as both a port regulator and a service provider. APA is an industrial and commercial public institution in charge of operating, managing, and promoting the port facilities in Abidjan, Treichville.
Importers & Exporters	Business Manager	Export or Import finished and semi-finished goods for local consumption and raw materials for manufacturing.
Stevedore Company	Director of Operations	It is an occupation that involves cargo operations, i.e., loading and unloading cargo on ships. It also includes various other dockside functions.
Commercial bank	Operations Manager	-Primary functions include accepting deposits, granting loans, advances, cash, credit, overdraft, and discounting bills. -Secondary functions include issuing letters of credit, undertaking safe custody of valuables, providing consumer finance, educational loans, etc.
SWS Subject matter expert	Independent Expert in SWS.	Somebody who has deep knowledge of the functionality of the Ivorian SWS and years of experience in the field.

Insurance company	Manager	They provide insurance cover that relates to goods that are transported to and from Côte D'Ivoire through the port of Abidjan.

Appendix 2: Map of the port of Abidjan

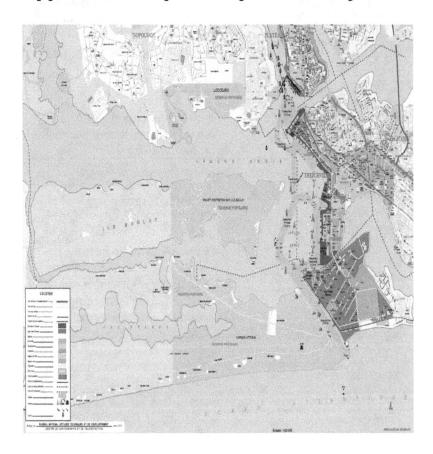

Appendix 3: Cote D'Ivoire Terminal

Côte d'Ivoire Terminal (CIT) is the second container terminal at the Port of Abidjan, operational since November 2022. It is the only terminal on Africa's west coast capable of accommodating vessels with a 16-meter draft, enhancing the port's competitiveness with an additional capacity of 1.5 million TEUs annually.

The terminal features six ship-to-shore gantry cranes, thirteen-yard cranes, and thirty-six terminal tractors — all electric — demonstrating a commitment to sustainable operations. Technological innovations include the implementation of the Navis® terminal operating system and a

Vehicle Booking System (VBS) for efficient truck scheduling. Technological innovations include the implementation of the Navis® terminal operating system and a Vehicle Booking System (VBS) for efficient truck scheduling.

CIT is also dedicated to environmental sustainability, aiming for EDGE (Excellence in Design for Greater Efficiency) certification for its administrative and maintenance buildings and pursuing ISO 9001, 14001, and 45001 certifications in its first year of operations.

Appendix 4: Abidjan Terminal

Abidjan Terminal, the first container terminal at the Port of Abidjan, features a quay length of approximately 1,000

meters and a draft of 11.5 meters. The terminal comprises five berths, with two berths (Nos. 21 and 22) measuring 320 meters in length and 11.5 meters in depth, and two additional berths (Nos. 23 and 24) extending 440 meters with a depth of 12.5 meters. The container yard spans 34 hectares, providing substantial space for container storage and handling. These specifications enable the terminal to accommodate vessels up to 260 meters in length with drafts not exceeding 11.5 meters.

Appendix 5: Vridi Canal

The Vridi Canal is a crucial maritime infrastructure in Côte d'Ivoire, forming the main maritime access route to the Port of Abidjan. It connects the Ébrié Lagoon to the Atlantic Ocean, enabling ocean-going vessels to access the port.

Technical Specifications (as of recent upgrades)

Length: Approximately 2.7 km

Width:

- Originally: around 70 meters
- After expansion (2015–2019 project): widened to 370 meters at the entrance

Depth:

- Originally: around 13.5 meters
- Now: 16 meters after dredging and deepening works (to accommodate Post-Panamax vessels)

Navigational Importance

- Allows access to one of the largest and busiest ports in West Africa.
- Supports the transit of containers, oil tankers, and bulk carriers.
- Handles vessels with a capacity of up to 100,000 DWT (deadweight tonnage).

Modernization

- In recent years, the canal underwent major widening and deepening works as part of a port expansion program.
- The objective: to enhance competitiveness and adapt to the evolution of global maritime trade (larger vessels).

Appendix 6: Port Information Template

6.1 Location

Considered one of the largest, most modern, and best-equipped ports in West Africa, the Port of Abidjan is located on a lagoon and connected to the sea by a buoyed channel 2.8 km in length and 13.0 m in depth. It lies at Longitude 4°00′ and Latitude 5°15′N.

Abidjan is the economic capital and main port of Côte d'Ivoire. The main export products include coffee, cocoa, cotton, timber, cashew nuts, palm oil, manganese, bananas, etc. Imports include machinery, steel, food products, vehicles, chemicals, and more.

Official working hours: 07:30–12:00 and 14:30–19:00

6.2 Navigation

Pilotage: Pilotage is compulsory through the Vridi Canal and is available both day and night. Vessels must inform the Harbor Master by VHF radio either 24 or 6 hours prior to arrival at the roadstead, providing fore and aft draft information. Vessels arriving at night must inform Port Control by 17:00 the previous day.

Pilots can be contacted on VHF channels 12 or 16. Vessels requiring a pilot should sound three long blasts on their whistle or siren. The pilot will board the vessel as soon as entry into the Vridi Canal is possible.

Vridi Channel Entrance Restrictions:

- Access to the Vridi Canal is subject to currents and tides.
- Maximum draft for entrance: 38 ft (11.50 m)
- Maximum draught is calculated at low tide.
- Water density: 1.012 – 1.015 (brackish water).

6.3 Berths Post Description

Map reference number	Length (m) and Description	Draught (m)	Other Restrictions	Observations
North Quay (1 to 5) General Cargo	775m /quays	31'/9.45 m	Warships priority on berths 4 & 5	Wheat vessels have priority on Berth Number 1 and 3
West Quay (6 to 13) General Cargo	1,525 m/quays	31'/9.45 m		
West quay (14 & 14bis) Mineral + Manganese		9.45m		Clinker, cement
South quay (16 to 20) Quay 16 = Palm oil		36'/11m	Priority to Roro / Palm oil tankers	48 hours' notice is required from vessels wishing to use this facility
Quay 17 = General cargo + Palm oil				
Quay 18 to 20 = Roro Terminal (Length of slope abt 17.50 m / Height of slope abt 1.50 m)				

South Quay (21 to 22) Container ships	> 1,785 m/quay	36' /11 m		
South Quay (23 to 24) Container ships	390m	38' / 11.50 m		
South Quay (25) Container ships	Max LOA 190 m	38' / 11.50 m	Bow thruster required	
Fishing port (fishing boat)		23' /7.01 m		
Banana quay	310 m	7 m	Reefer cargo only	Reefer cargo only
Siveng (Bulk fertilizer)	Max 155 m	27'/ 8.20 m	Fertilizer berth	
CNR / PHILIPS	Max 120 m	6.50 m	Private berth	
SOCOPAO (private berth)		21' /6.50 m	Private berth	

6.4 Tanker Berths

Map Ref	Description	Length (m)	Draught (m)	Other Restrictions	Observations
1	PETRO CI – Tanker Berth	Max 200	10.06 (33')	Max beam: 32.20 m; Displacement: 40,000 MT	Wheat vessels have been accommodated

2	SIAP – Tanker Berth	Max 180	9.45 (31')	Max beam: 32.20 m; Displacement: 35,000 MT	
3	SIR I – Tanker (CBM)	–	9.45	Max DWT: 80,000 MT; Cargo: Crude Oil; Hoses: 12 inches	Berthing by day only, time fixed by the chief pilot; Beacon: IMODCO – 2 flashes every 6 seconds
4	SIR II – Tanker (SPM)	Min 200	21 (69')	Max DWT: 250,000 MT; Cargo: Crude Oil; Hoses: 16 inches	Berthing before 16:00 GMT/LT; Beacon: IMODCO – flash every 2 seconds; Sailing permitted anytime
5	PETRO CI Soutes – Tanker Berth	Max 145	10	–	–

6	Map reference number and Espoir terminal (Offshore): The FPSO is a floating production, storage, and off-loading vessel located in territorial waters off the coast of Ivory Coast, West Africa. No draft limitations. The FPSO is a converted 155,000 DWT tanker registered under the Panamanian flag and has an overall length of 280m. The loaded draft is 15.30m.
7	Baobab Marine Terminal (Offshore): The Baobab marine terminal consists of the 346,000 DWT Floating Production, Storage, and Offloading vessel ("FPSO"). Baobab Ivoirien MV 10, including its bow mooring, hoses, pipeline, and manifold pipeline from the production manifolds and all waters surrounding the FPSO Baobab Ivoirian MV 10 within the two (2) nautical miles radius.

6.5 Requested Documents When the Vessel Will Berth In Port Only

For boarding formalities, the captain is to prepare the following documents:

- Arms and Ammunition – 7 copies
- Dangerous Cargo Declaration – 2 copies
- Port of Call List (with security level for each) – 7 copies

- Paints, Thinners, Chemicals, Grease, Luboils – 7 copies
- Crew List – 7 copies
- Personal Effects – 2 copies
- Passenger List – 7 copies
- Stowaway List – 4 copies
- Stores List – 7 copies
- Cargo Manifest – 7 copies
- Animal List – 7 copies
- Narcotics List – 2 copies
- Vaccination List – 2 copies
- Bunkers List – 2 copies
- Alcohol, Cigarettes, etc. – 2 copies
- Health Declaration – 2 copies
- Parcel List (mail, packages, etc.) – 7 copies

6.6 Fresh Water

Available at any time at the quayside via pipe connection or by barge at anchorage.

6.7 Bunkers

Available by barge at anchorage.

At quay: Available at the tanker terminal via pipe connection.

6.8 Provisions / Stores and Others

Fresh provisions are available on request, with no limitations. About 80 ship chandlers are available at any time.

6.9 Repairs

All types of repairs are available and conducted by CARENA. Diver and underwater repairs are also available. Floating docks with lifting capacities from 2,000 tons and up can accommodate vessels up to 83 meters in length. Power capacity includes 380V and 440V at 50 Hz, or 60 to 300 KVA. Fire circuits, fresh water circuits, compressed air, and fuel storage tanks are supported by 10 cranes capable of lifting up to 100 tons. In partnership with "SAGA Lifting," it is possible to lift 80 tons at 21 meters.

6.10 Other Restrictions

During Christian or Muslim holidays, it may be difficult to obtain gangs for daytime operations. Therefore, Owners/Charterers are requested to notify stevedores in advance to ensure preparation.